MOUNTAIN BIKING

Paul Mason

HODDER
Wayland

An imprint of Hodder Children's Books

to the limit

MOUNTAIN BIKING

Other titles in this well-cool series are:

BLADING
MOTOCROSS
SKATEBOARDING
SNOWBOARDING
SURFING

Grateful thanks to *mbr* magazine for supplying photos.

Prepared for Hodder Wayland by Roger Coote Publishing, Gissings Farm, Fressingfield, Eye, Suffolk IP21 5SH

© Hodder Wayland 2000

Project Management: Mason Editorial Services
Designer: Tim Mayer

Published in 2000 by
Hodder Wayland, an imprint of
Hodder Children's Books

ISBN 0 7502 3061 4

Printed and bound in Italy by G. Canale C.S.p.A., Turin

Hodder Children's Books
A division of Hodder Headline Ltd
338 Euston Road, London NW1 3BH

RDPII   17   16A

WARNING!
Mountain biking is a dangerous sport. This book is full of advice, but reading it won't keep you safe on the mountain. Take responsibility for your own safety.

WHAT IS MOUNTAIN BIKING?

Mountain biking's thrills are summed up by the excitement of racing at top speed down a trail that's only wide enough for one rider, trying to catch up to your disappearing friend (or trying to stay ahead of a friend who's desperately trying to catch you).

This kind of single-track riding, as it's called, is sought out by mountain bikers all round the world. But there are plenty of other thrills in mountain biking, of course. There are jumps, downhill rides, cross country, dual slalom races, 24-hour relay races. . . in fact, too many different kinds of mountain-bike activity to list here.

Bikers enjoying a day far from the city.

The Secret Language of Mountain Biking

Drop-off — A vertical or near-vertical descent.

Dual slalom — Where two riders race side-by-side down a pre-set course.

Fire road — A wide track through a forest, originally built as access for large trucks or fire fighters.

Freeride — Riding anywhere you want to; usually freeriders try to take the most extreme routes possible.

Full-sus — Short for full suspension: a bike that has suspension for the front and rear wheels.

Hardtail — A bike with suspension forks on the front but a rigid rear.

Travel — The amount of movement in a suspension system: a bike whose forks move 80mm would be said to have 80mm travel.

Trials — Where riders perform tricks on their bikes while moving around a pre-arranged set of obstacles.

'Mountain biking is about freedom. It's about escape and adventure. . . When you get to the end of the trail and look back, you say to yourself, "Whoa! I just did that." It's a real adrenaline rush.' Gary Klein, mountain-bike pioneer, explains why he got into the sport in the first place.

Back When It All Began

Mountain biking started in California. A group of friends got together a bunch of old beach cruisers and drove up to the top of their local mountain with the bikes in a pickup truck. Then they raced each other back down again. 'This is fun: let's do it again!' they thought, and mountain biking had been born. The sport spread and spread, until twenty years or so after that first run there were more mountain bikes being sold than any other kind.

"A thoroughly useful maintenance manual that also happens to be great fun to read."
— Jim Langley, *Bicycling magazine*

2ND EDITION

ZINN and the ART of MOUNTAIN BIKE MAINTENANCE

By Lennard Zinn
Senior Technical Writer of VeloNews

The Godfathers of Mountain Biking

The Californian youngsters who first started mountain biking realised the bikes they had been using weren't really that good. Some of them started building their own bikes. Today, these are some of the biggest names in the mountain biking industry: Gary Fisher, Keith Bontrager, Tom Ritchey and Gary Klein have all given their names to successful companies.

Jargon-buster

Coaster brakes Brakes that are part of the back wheel: you pedal backwards to slow down.

Beach cruiser A relaxed style of bike with no gears, coaster brakes and big, fat tyres.

The bikes have changed since the early days of mountain biking, but the thrill is the same.

Taiwan

Most of the world's mountain bike factories are Taiwanese. Over half of the world's mountain bike frames are currently built there, and many of the components too. Taiwan has begun to face stiff competition from China, though, and may lose the number-one spot before long.

Hardtail heaven

Most people, in most places, ride a hardtail bike. They have suspension forks on the front, but no travel at the rear. Why are these bikes so popular?

- 'They're cheaper.' Hardtails are easier to build and there are less components. You get more bike for your money.
- 'You know they work.' The designs have been developed over decades, so with very few exceptions hardtails work well.
- 'They're quicker.' Hardtails used to be thought quicker than full-suspension bikes over varied ground; many people argue that this isn't true any more.

The biggest difference, though, is that the riding experience on a hardtail is more immediate: you can really feel the ground under you. You have to concentrate harder: hit a rock in the middle of the trail and it'll probably knock you off. This can seem exciting or dangerous, depending on your attitude: it boils down to personal choice.

Groupset: 24 or 27 gears. Some riders just have one ring on the front, and 8 or 9 gears. A few people even ride fixed-wheel, single-speed bikes.

What's In A Frame?

Frames are made out of loads of different materials, but the three main ones are:

Steel Less popular now, but a strong frame material that 'gives' a little under stress.

Aluminium 6061 and 7005 are the most common types. Aluminium bikes have a stiff, harsh ride, and are more expensive but lighter than steel.

Titanium The most expensive of these three frame materials, but very popular with those who can afford it.

Typical modern hardtail

Angled top tube: makes it less painful if you fall off!

Short stem: gives an easier riding position and more control.

Wide riser bars: more control and a more relaxed riding position.

Aluminium frame: 6061 or 7005 are the most common grades.

Aheadset: allows quick changing of forks and easy maintenance.

Pedals: clipless or flat – personal choice.

Lightweight wheels: heavier wheels are used for downhill.

V-brakes: some bikes have disc brakes, which are more powerful, but V-brakes are lighter and stop the bike well.

Suspension forks: between 60mm and 120mm travel.

9

Full Suspension

Today you're more likely to meet a full-suspension bike out on the trail than ever before. But they used to be ridden only by downhill freaks. So what changed: why are full-sus bikes so popular now?

- Cross-country full-suspension bikes are now super-light: maybe two or three pounds heavier than an equivalent hardtail, instead of ten pounds or more.
- Fans of full suspension argue that the increased grip given by the suspension makes them faster even though they're a little heavier.
- The designs have been worked through: they're efficient and you can buy from well-known companies with confidence that the bike will work.
- They're more comfortable to ride for a whole day.

How to choose

Here are a few guidelines that could help you choose your first full-suspension bike:

- Pick a bike made by a well-known company, ideally one whose bikes you've ridden before and liked.
- Choose a simple design which you can set up and ride without fiddling with it all the time.
- Make sure you test-ride the bike. Any good shop will let you do this: some even have off-road areas you can use.

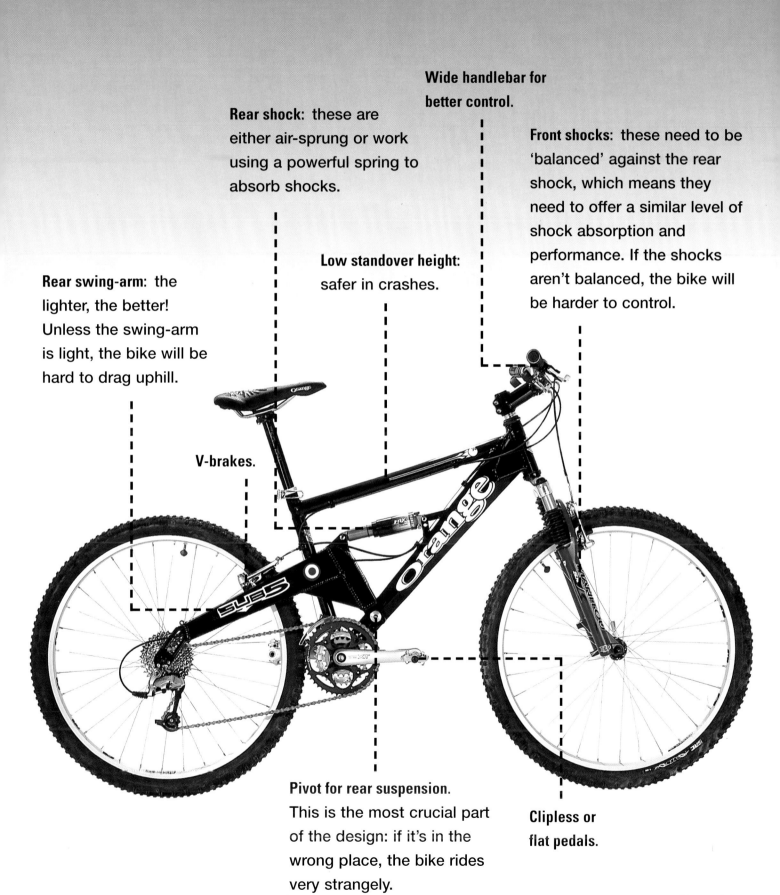

Rear shock: these are either air-sprung or work using a powerful spring to absorb shocks.

Wide handlebar for better control.

Front shocks: these need to be 'balanced' against the rear shock, which means they need to offer a similar level of shock absorption and performance. If the shocks aren't balanced, the bike will be harder to control.

Rear swing-arm: the lighter, the better! Unless the swing-arm is light, the bike will be hard to drag uphill.

Low standover height: safer in crashes.

V-brakes.

Pivot for rear suspension. This is the most crucial part of the design: if it's in the wrong place, the bike rides very strangely.

Clipless or flat pedals.

11

RIDING:
Freeride

Just let the bike go. Faster! Faster!

All 'freeriding' means is just getting out on your bike and riding over, around or through whatever you meet. You can ride downhill, uphill, down drop-offs, through singletrack, on fire roads or your local trails, 50 miles from home – it's all freeride.

Freeride checklist

- ☑ Water bottle or water-carrying backpack.
- ☑ Waterproof top.
- ☑ Warm clothes – fleece is best as it doesn't absorb water.
- ☑ Tools – at *least*: puncture kit, spare inner tube, chain splitter, tyre levers, allen keys.
- ☑ Sunscreen, if you're going out on a sunny day.
- ☑ Warm gloves and a hat that fits under your helmet, if it's cold.

What makes this kind of riding different is the attitude that the riders carry with them in their heads. This can best be summed up in one word: extreme. If you're out freeriding, you're not out for a quiet day in the countryside. You're chasing the biggest adrenaline rush you can find, looking for the fastest, steepest and most difficult routes.

Jargon buster

Single track A trail wide enough to fit one bike, and only one bike, at a time. Very exciting to ride: you often can't see far ahead, obstacles jut out into your path, and you're constantly having to react to the route.

What to ride

There isn't a particular kind of bike for freeriding, though almost all bikes have front suspension. The most important thing is to be sure your bike is strong and safe: if you're riding fast, scary routes you don't want your bike to break!

Downhill

The thrill of charging full-speed through a narrow lane in the trees, or across the steep, open slope of a mountain, is as exhilarating as snowboarding down a steep slope or surfing in big waves. Welcome to downhill mountain biking.

Many downhill bikers live in ski resorts through the summer. There are two reasons for this. The first is that ski slopes without snow on them make perfect mountain-bike trails. The second is the lifts. Downhill bikes have huge amounts of travel and are very, very heavy, to give them added traction. They're so heavy that they're almost impossible to ride uphill: unless you live near a ski lift, you're in for a lot of pushing!

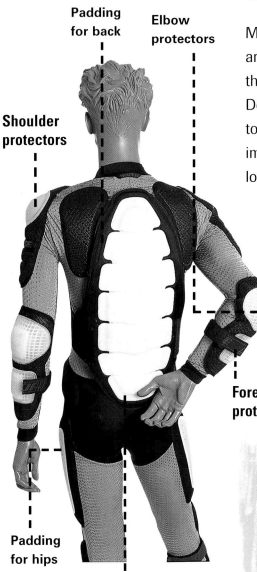

Padding for back

Elbow protectors

Shoulder protectors

Forearm protectors

Padding for hips

Hard plastic plates protect torso.

Anne-Caroline Chausson

The French downhill star won her 7th world-champion's jersey in 1999 at Are, Sweden. 'Each year I have more to lose than the others. Each year I think it's time to go out and get my jersey, and the pressure is greater, especially this year as I have a new team. I was very, very stressed before this race,' she said after winning by 1.61 secs from Katja Repo of Finland.

WARNING!

Downhilling is potentially very dangerous. Riders often walk their route several times before going down it on a bike, and they wear full body armour and full-face helmets in case they crash. Anyone who thinks they can ride downhill courses without planning the route carefully is likely to end up badly hurt.

Dual Slalom

Dual slalom is like racing your friend around the local woods, except you might win a cup at the end.

'Real' dual racing involves two riders trying to beat each other to the bottom of a pre-set course. They start together and try to make it through the twists and turns as quickly as possible. Dual courses usually feature jumps, which are sometimes specially built 'doubles' – two humps of earth designed to allow the most daredevil riders to jump the gap between them.

Brian Lopes – King of Dual

One of the world's best dual riders is Brian Lopes from the U.S.A. As the commentators at 1998 World Championships said: 'His acceleration is unparalleled in the sport of cycling: this guy drives it like nobody else.'

Of course, you don't need a specially prepared course and an organized event to race dual slalom: a local trail that's wide enough for two bikes will do. Get together a group of friends and take it in turns to race each other down the trail. One of you rides on the left-hand side, the other on the right: first one down races the winner of the next race.

Dual rules

If you're planning to go out with your friends and set up a dual race, there are a few things you should remember:

- Everyone has the right to use public trails. Make *sure* there's no one using the route you're racing over. This means you must be able to see the whole route from the top, as well as anywhere that people might enter the route.

- Only race on trails where bike riders are legally allowed.

- If the trail is on private land, you *must* get the owner's permission before racing on it.

- Wear a helmet!

Dual riders show no mercy to their opponents on the course, but share a joke after the race.

RIDING: Urban Freeride

Fancy riding sideways along a wall? Up and down a tree trunk? Or maybe hopping between two picnic tables is your thing. . . whatever, this is the crazy world of urban freeriding.

Urban freeriders look at the landscape in the same way as skateboarders: every obstacle becomes an opportunity to perform a trick. Stairs are there to be ridden down; park benches to be jumped; walls to bunny hop; narrow alleys to be wheelied. One thing that's important, though, is showing consideration for other people. However much fun you're having, make sure you're not ruining someone else's day by riding your bike in an inappropriate place.

Alec Liell: No-footed endo.

Chris Jones: Subway step leap.

James McLintic: Lip-hop cross-up.

Gavin Cummings: Manual to kerb hop.

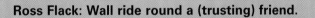

Ross Flack: Wall ride round a (trusting) friend.

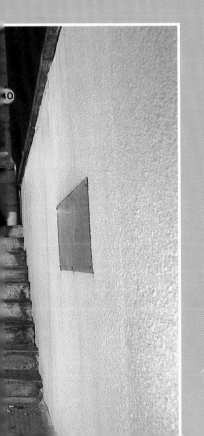

TECHNIQUE
hills

Different riders have very different riding styles: some are super-smooth, others seem to wrestle their bikes up and down hills as though they're in a fight. Most people, of course, fall somewhere between the two. Whatever your riding style, whether you're going uphill or down there are a few tips that help even the best riders go faster.

Uphill

DO – Try to stay sitting down on steep slopes: it gives good grip and smooth acceleration.

DON'T – Stand out of the saddle and push hard on the pedals: the back wheel will slide around and you'll tire very quickly.

DO – Keep your weight balanced over the bike: lean into the slope and bend your arms to stop the front wheel lifting up.

DON'T – Pull back hard on the handlebars to try and put power into your pedalling: you'll do a wheelie and land on your back.

How to do it, shown above, and how not to do it, most definitely shown on the right.

Downhill

DO – Wear something to stop your eyes filling with tears: then you'll be able to see where you're going, which is good.

DO – Keep a firm grip on the handlebars.

DON'T – Try to change gear in a bumpy or twisty downhill section: next thing you know you'll be lying in the bushes wondering if anything is broken.

DO – Keep your weight centred on the bike: this means shifting it backwards through steeper sections. Both wheels will then grip evenly.

DON'T – Put your weight forwards: you might go flying over the handlebars if you hit anything.

DO – Control your speed going into tricky areas or places where you can't see what's ahead.

DON'T – Assume that what's ahead will be as easy as what you're riding now.

TECHNIQUE jumping

Deliberately trying to leave the ground on a bicycle, which after all is mainly designed to stay on the ground, sounds like a pretty stupid thing to do. But it can make your riding safer: sometimes it's much better to leap over a difficult patch of ground than it is to ride across it. To be able to do this you have to practise. Try jumping off little curbs and drop-offs that you could easily ride down first, before building up to larger obstacles.

3 Land smoothly, with a big smile.

2 Let the back wheel follow the front off the ground.

1 Lift the front wheel.

Some riders/crazies make jumping their main aim. These riders perform tricks with names like no-footer, no-handed seat grab and, best of all, suicide air. Jumping crazies will risk life and limb to provide a spectacular picture (as you can see from the photos).

WARNING

Jumping is DANGEROUS. Take great care if you decide you want to try to learn, and get help from someone who knows what they're doing.

COMPETITIONS

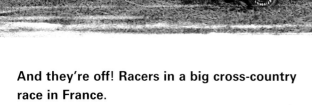

And they're off! Racers in a big cross-country race in France.

As in any sport, mountain bikers have always been keen to try to find out who's the best, and competition has always been part of the mountain bike scene. There are local, regional and international races in lots of disciplines. Cross-country, downhill, dual slalom, trials, jumping. . . if you can put a name to it, there's a competition for it somewhere. Cross-country is even part of the Olympics.

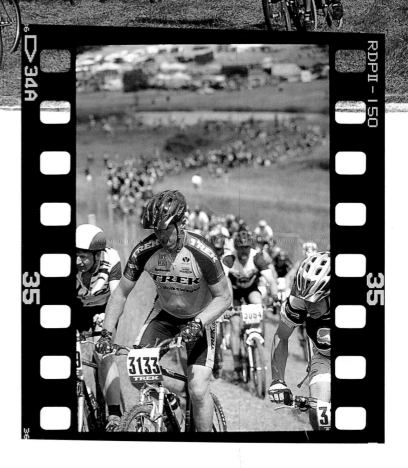

Recently there has been a growth of 'alternative' competitions, which are a little different from the traditional ones. Among the most popular of these is the 24-hour marathon race, where teams of riders race in relays for 24 hours: whichever team has gone furthest in the time is the winner. Also increasing in popularity are adventure-racing triathlons, where competitors do an open-water swim, a mountain-bike ride and a cross-country run.

Michael Rasmussen

Michael Rasmussen of Denmark speaks 7 languages: German, English, Danish, Spanish, Italian, Swedish and Norwegian. He answered press conference questions in each after he won the world cross-country championships in Are, Sweden. 'It's a very beautiful and unique tradition in sport to have the world champion's jersey, so it has always been my dream,' he said after his win.

Mud-man racer looks glad to have finished.

A running start to a 24-hour relay race.

The World's fastest rider

Mountain biking's fastest superstar is undoubtedly Nicolas Vouilloz of France, known around the world as 'Nico'. Going into the 1999 world championships (held in Are, Sweden in late 1999) Nico had already won seven junior and senior world championship medals. One of his main rivals, Steve Peat of England, was forced to pull out before the race, but Nico was still faced with one of the hardest competitions ever. It went something like this:

Early descents: Americans Brian Lopes and Shaums March are fastest of the early racers, setting good times.

Later riders: David Vazquez (Spain) crosses the line in a blisteringly fast 5.14. Then Shaun Palmer (U.S.A.) races like a superhuman: he seems about to take first place, but slides on the tarmac at the finish and crashes. Whoops!

Final riders: Nico hits the course. He rides smoother than anyone else, and crosses the line 10 seconds faster. A shiver goes down the backs of the riders still waiting to race: this looks like an unbeatable time. Only Mickael Pascal (France) and Eric Carter (U.S.A.) get close, taking second and third. Nico has won his *eighth* world downhill championship.

Still want to become a professional?

Nicolas Vouilloz is the most successful rider ever in downhill, which is the most popular and visually exciting form of mountain biking. But in 1999 he lost his sponsor, Sunn, and had to enter races without a team backup and without being paid.

However good you are, being a professional mountain biker is not an easy way to earn a living.

'It's incredible to win here,' Nico said after winning in Sweden. 'The track was very slow at the top and I was just happy to stay on the bike; I was convinced Mickael would beat me.' He's entered eight world championships and won eight: you have to wonder, can anyone beat Nico?

Ethics and Safety

All this high-octane fun is great, but unless you're on a race course you're probably sharing your riding area with other outdoor enthusiasts. There are certain things you need to do to make sure you don't ruin their fun: it can be quite shocking to have a mountain bike whizz past at 30 mph when you're out for a quiet day in the country.

Mountain bikers already have a bad reputation, especially with walkers. Only by being extra-polite can we start to change this. If you think it doesn't matter, you're wrong: if mountain bikers continue to be seen as dangerous and selfish trail users, they will end up being banned from more and more places. In the end, there won't be anywhere good to ride.

Safety checklist

See the box in the Freeride section, on page 12–13, for a list of things you should take out biking with you.

Good image advice

- Only ride where you're allowed to.

- Always slow down or stop for walkers and horses to avoid scaring them: it's easy to get back up to speed again afterwards.

- Greet people you meet with a smile, and thank anyone who stops for you or opens a gate.

- It's a good idea to have a bell on your bike, to warn people you're about to overtake them. If you don't have a bell, a polite 'Excuse me' or 'Watch out' will do.

Specially signposted routes for mountain bikes (VTT stands for bikes for all terrain in French) in the Alps.

Enviro biking

Bicycles are good for the environment, right? Well, yes and no. They don't use fossil fuels that cause pollution, but they can have a negative effect. Everyone who uses the outdoors – bikers, walkers, runners, horses – wears away a little soil as they pass. Mountain bikes aren't the worst offenders at this, but there are a couple of things you can do to cut down the amount of soil erosion you cause:

1 Stick to marked trails, so that erosion can be controlled by those who manage the trail.

2 Try not to skid your bike: the sliding tyre rips grass and soil loose.

How not to do it: that dust is soil, which will be blown away in the wind.

Glossary

Word:	Means:	Doesn't Mean:
Adrenaline	A hormone produced by your body in exciting circumstances.	A Baltic Shipping Company.
BMX	Short for bicycle motocross.	Billy's Mum's Cross.
Bunny hop	A small jump used by mountain bikers to clear obstacles.	Jump by little animal with white tail.
Clipless pedals	Pedals that attach to the sole of your shoe using a clamp.	(Strangely) pedals without clips, since they do clip to your feet. Hmm.
Motocross	Motorcycle racing around a specially prepared off-road course.	Annoyed garage owner.
Shock	A suspension unit that allows the wheels to move up and down under pressure.	Fright caused by mountain biker zooming past.
Ski lift	A lift that transports skiers up the slopes of a mountain. The most common kinds are chairs strung from a cable and enclosed cabins.	Manoeuvre by mountain-based weight lifters.
Sponsor	Someone or something who pays a sportsperson to enter competition, in return for publicity.	A rash caused by spon.
Transplant	Move something from one place to another. Someone who moves from one city to another might be said to have transplanted their lives.	Addition of hair to bald person's head.
Wheelie	Riding along with the front wheel of your bike in the air.	Man with head shaped like wheel.

Further Information

Books to read

The only other recent mountain biking book especially for young people is Extreme Sports: *Mountain Biking* (Franklin Watts, 1998). There are some good general books available: outdoor equipment shops, bike shops and specialist travel bookshops will have a range of books about bike maintenance and where to ride.

Magazines

There are lots of mountain biking magazines: two of the best are *mbr* and *Mountain Biking UK*. The photos in this book were supplied by *mbr*.

The Internet

There are plenty of places to buy things on the internet, and almost all manufacturers have a web site where you can find out about their products.

1999 World Champions

Event	Winner	(Country)
Espoir Cross Country, Men	Marco Bui	(Italy)
Junior Cross Country, Men	Nicolas Filippi	(France)
Junior Cross Country, Women	Anna Szafraniec	(Poland)
Junior Downhill, Men	Nathan Rennie	(Australia)
Junior Downhill, Women	Sabrina Jonnier	(France)
Senior Cross Country, Men	Michael Rasmussen	(Denmark)
Senior Cross Country, Women	Margarita Fullana	(Spain)
Senior Downhill, Men	Nicolas Vouilloz	(France)
Senior Downhill, Women	Anne-Caroline Chausson	(France)

Index

Picture Acknowlegements

The publishers would like to thank the following for giving their permission for photos to be used in this book: All photos supplied by John Kitchiner/mbr magazine.